D1200562

Long, Short, High, Low, Thin, Wide

Long, Short,

Thomas Y. Crowell Company • **New York**

8 49 50 51 52 53 54 55 56 57 58 59

High, Low, Thin, Wide

By James T. Fey

Illustrated by Janie Russell

YOUNG MATH BOOKS

Edited by Dr. Max Beberman, Director of the Committee
on School Mathematics Projects, University of Illinois

BIGGER AND SMALLER
by Robert Froman

CIRCLES
by Mindel and Harry Sitomer

THE ELLIPSE
by Mannis Charosh

ESTIMATION
by Charles F. Linn

FRACTIONS ARE PARTS OF THINGS
by J. Richard Dennis

GRAPH GAMES
by Frédérique and Papy

LONG, SHORT, HIGH, LOW, THIN, WIDE
by James T. Fey

ODDS AND EVENS
by Thomas C. O'Brien

STRAIGHT LINES, PARALLEL LINES,
PERPENDICULAR LINES
by Mannis Charosh

WEIGHING & BALANCING
by Jane Jonas Srivastava

WHAT IS SYMMETRY?
by Mindel and Harry Sitomer

L.C. Card 75-158705
ISBN 0-690-50549-3
0-690-50550-7 (LB)
2   3   4   5   6   7   8   9   10

Long,
Short,
High,
Low,
Thin,
Wide

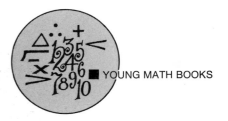

■ YOUNG MATH BOOKS

Have you ever wondered:

How tall am I?

How high can I reach?

How long is the string on my kite?

How high is the ceiling in my house?

How wide is the playground?

You can answer questions that ask how tall, how short, how long, how high, or how wide things are by measuring.

Of course, if someone asked you, "How long is your pencil?" you could say, "My pencil is longer than my thumb."

Or you could say, "My pencil is shorter than my belt."

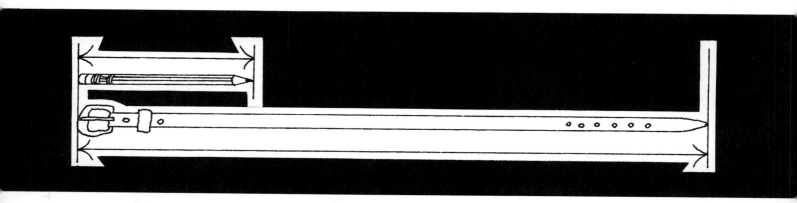

This is not a very careful way to measure. It tells a little about the length of your pencil. The pencil is longer than your thumb, but shorter than your belt.

But it doesn't really tell just how long your pencil is. The pencil could be a very long one, almost as long as your belt. Or it could be a very short pencil, just a little bit longer than your thumb.

A better way to describe the length of your pencil is to compare it with the length of a toothpick. Since most people know about how long a toothpick is, they will understand you if you say, "My pencil is longer than 2 toothpicks, but shorter than 3 toothpicks."

Put toothpicks end to end next to your pencil. Be sure that one end of the first toothpick is even with the eraser end of the pencil.

How long is the pencil in the picture?

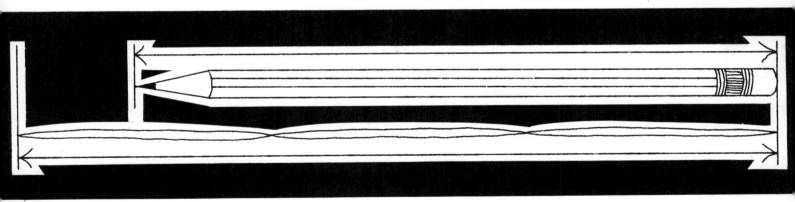

The pencil is longer than 2 toothpicks, but shorter than 3 toothpicks.

How long is *your* pencil?

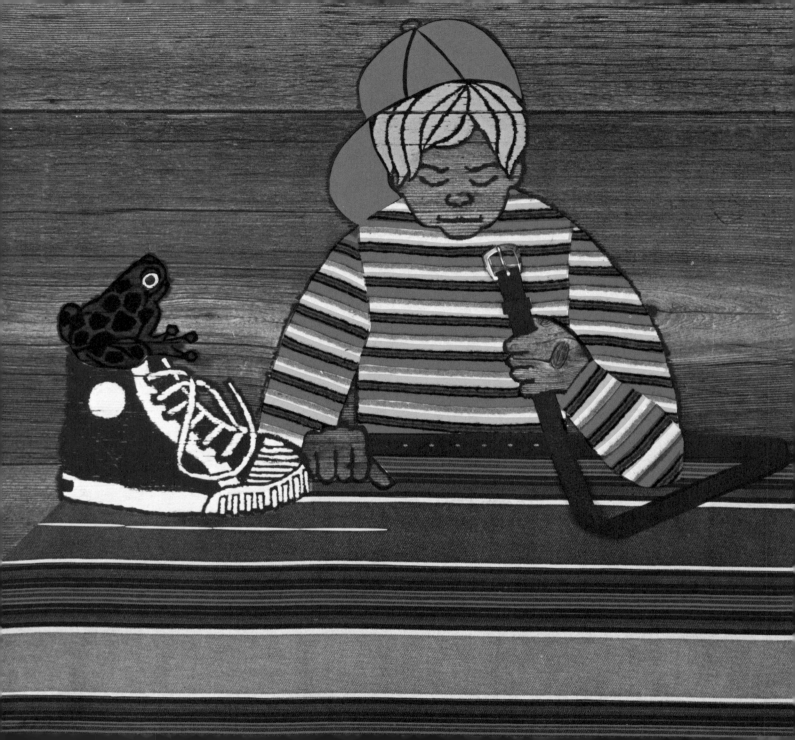

Now find the length of your shoe.

Place your shoe on a table so that the heel of the shoe is even with the edge of the table. Then carefully put toothpicks end to end next to the shoe.

The shoe in the picture is longer than 3 toothpicks, but shorter than 4.

How long is *your* shoe?

Find the length of your belt in the same way.

Stretch your hand out as far as you can. Then trace around it on a piece of paper. Now lay toothpicks end to end on the paper, in a line from the tip of your thumb to the tip of your little finger. This distance is called the span of your hand.

The hand in the picture is wider than 2 toothpicks, but not as wide as 3 toothpicks.

How wide is *your* hand?

To find out the length of your pencil, your belt, and your shoe, and the width of your hand span, you used the length of a toothpick as your UNIT OF MEASURE.

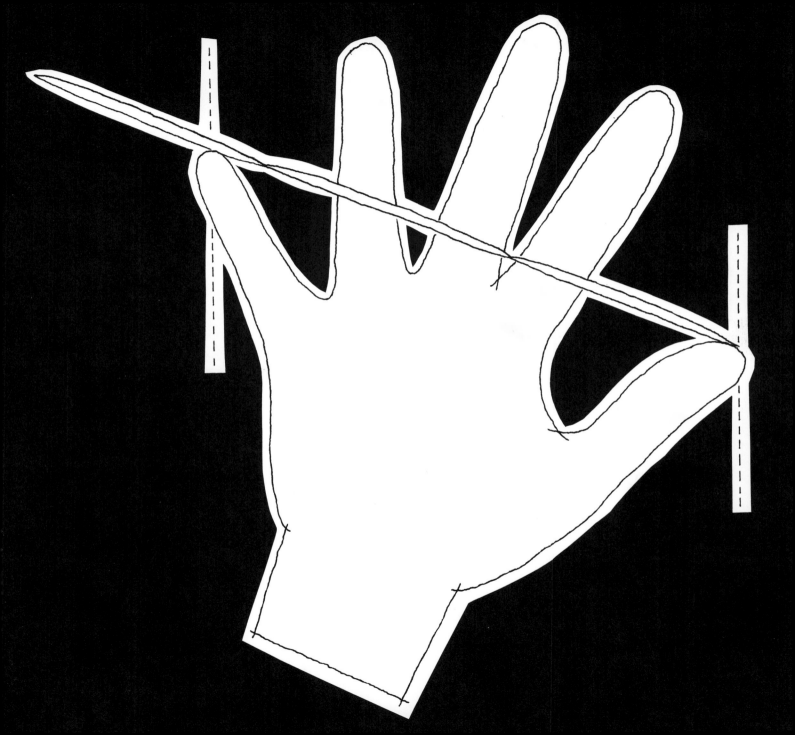

Toothpicks are not the only units of measure you can use. You can also use paper clips, bottle caps, ice cream sticks, pennies, or many other things. You just have to make sure that all the paper clips (or whatever unit of measure you use) are exactly the same size.

How may bottle caps long is your pencil?

Toothpicks, bottle caps, and pennies can all be helpful in telling how long things are. But it takes a long time to count a line of toothpicks as long as your belt. What if you wanted to find the length or width of your bedroom using toothpicks or pennies? Wouldn't that be a difficult job!

It is easier to find the length of an object much larger than a pencil or your hand if you choose a large unit of measure.

Try using your shoes.

The bed in the picture is longer than 7 shoes, but shorter than 8 shoes. Use *your* shoe to find the length of your bed.

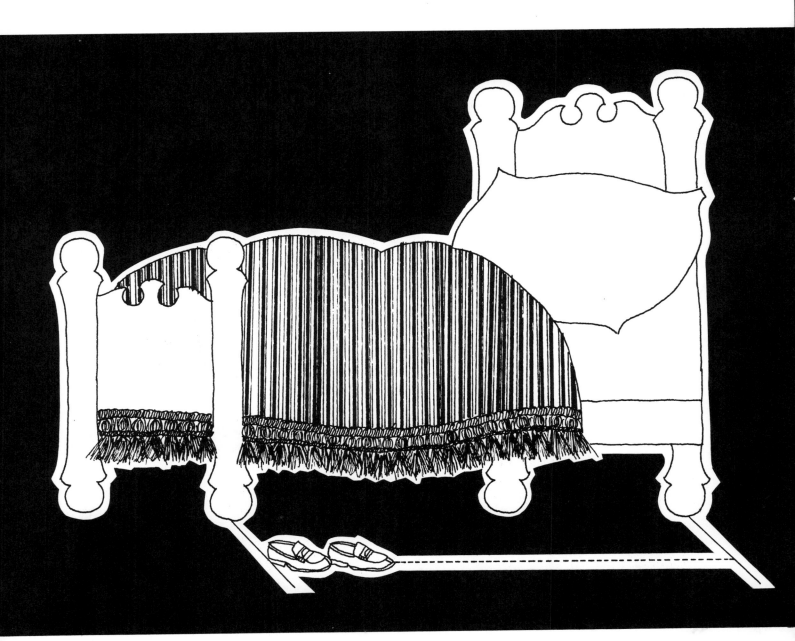

Stand with the heel of one shoe even with an end of the bed. Put the heel of your other shoe against the toe of the first. Then move the first shoe in front of the second, and continue this way until you reach the other end of the bed. How many shoes long is your bed?

How many shoes long is your bedroom? How many shoes long is it from the kitchen to your bedroom?

Now measure the same distances using different shoes.

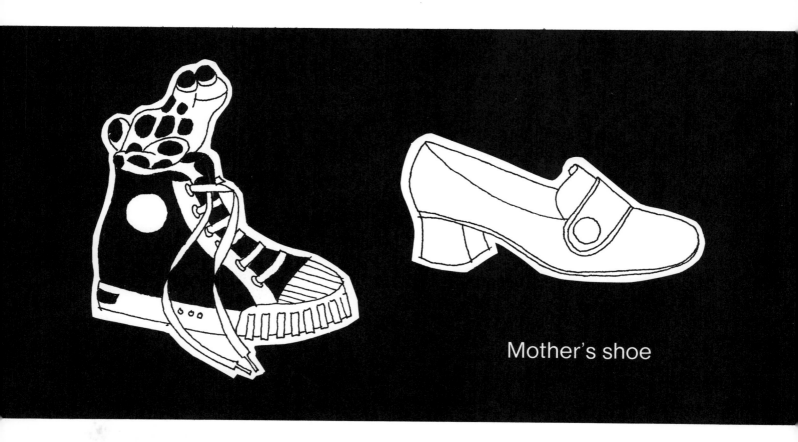

Mother's shoe

Did you notice that when you used your father's shoe, the bed was not as many shoes long as when you used your own shoe? When you used a baby's shoe, the bed was many more shoes long!

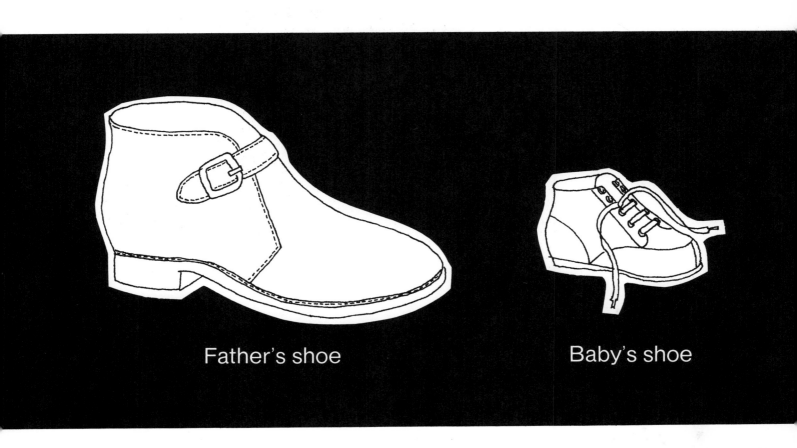

Father's shoe

Baby's shoe

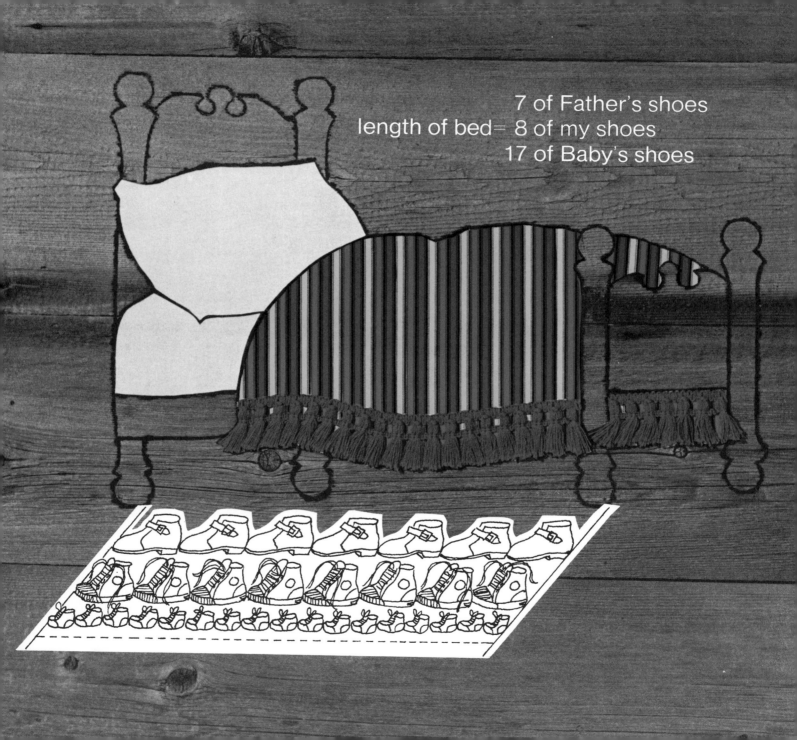

7 of Father's shoes

length of bed= 8 of my shoes

17 of Baby's shoes

Not all shoes are the same length. If you wanted to tell someone how long your bed was, you would have to say:

"My bed is 7 of my father's shoes long."

or

"My bed is 8 of my shoes long."

or

"My bed is 17 of the baby's shoes long."

If you used a hand or an arm or a book as a unit of measure, you would have to do the same thing, since different hands, arms, and books are different lengths.

People have always had to find ways of measuring. Even in earliest times they wanted to know such things as how much cloth they needed for their clothes or how much land they needed to plow.

At first people measured things almost the same way you did when you measured your pencil and your belt. Instead of toothpicks, they probably used sticks or grains of corn. They also used units of measurement equal in length to parts of their body:

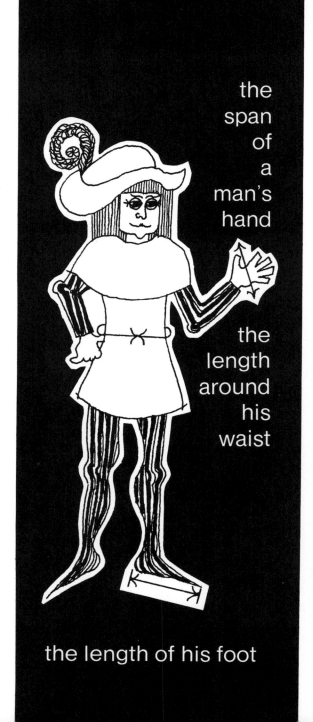

the span of a man's hand

the length around his waist

the length of his foot

But people soon learned that using many different objects as units of measurement often caused trouble.

For example, what if a man who wanted a new house built told the carpenter that his house must be "ten paces long and twenty paces wide." If the carpenter had shorter legs than the man, the house would not be as large as the buyer wanted.

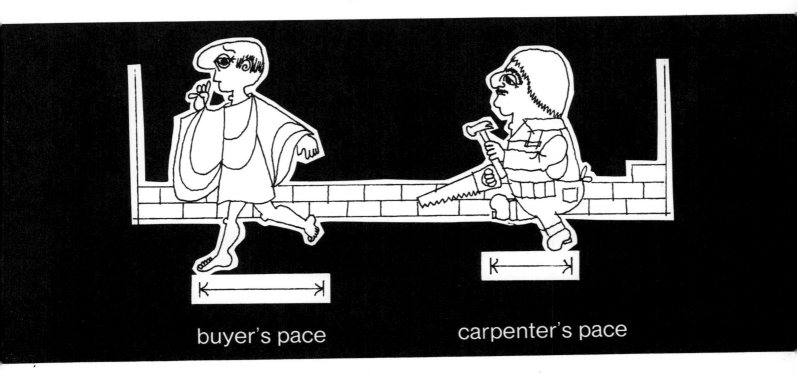

buyer's pace   carpenter's pace

1 palm

7 palms = 1 cubit

Something had to be done. There had to be units of measure that would always be the same.

The first known standard unit of measurement was the CUBIT. It was used in the Bible to tell the size of Noah's Ark. The Egyptians used the cubit as their basic measuring unit. A cubit was equal to the distance from a man's elbow to the tip of his middle finger.

For shorter measurements, the Egyptians used a PALM. A palm was the distance across 4 fingers. Seven palms equaled one cubit.

You might be thinking that palms and cubits are not better units of measure than paces, or shoes, or toothpicks. The Egyptian idea was to make standard cubit and palm measures.

The Egyptian kings had strips of wood or metal equal in length to the palm and cubit made into standard cubit rulers and standard palm rulers. The people could then use copies of these standard rulers to make sure that houses, clothes, and other things that were made for them were the sizes they had ordered.

The line segment in the picture is 1 palm long. Cut a string the same length as the line segment and use it to measure your pencil, your shoe, and your belt. How many palms long are they?

Egyptians found the cubit and palm helpful units for measuring. The ancient Greeks and Romans used still other units of measure. By about the year 1500 most people in Europe were using standard units based on measurements of parts of the body. Some of them are still used today.

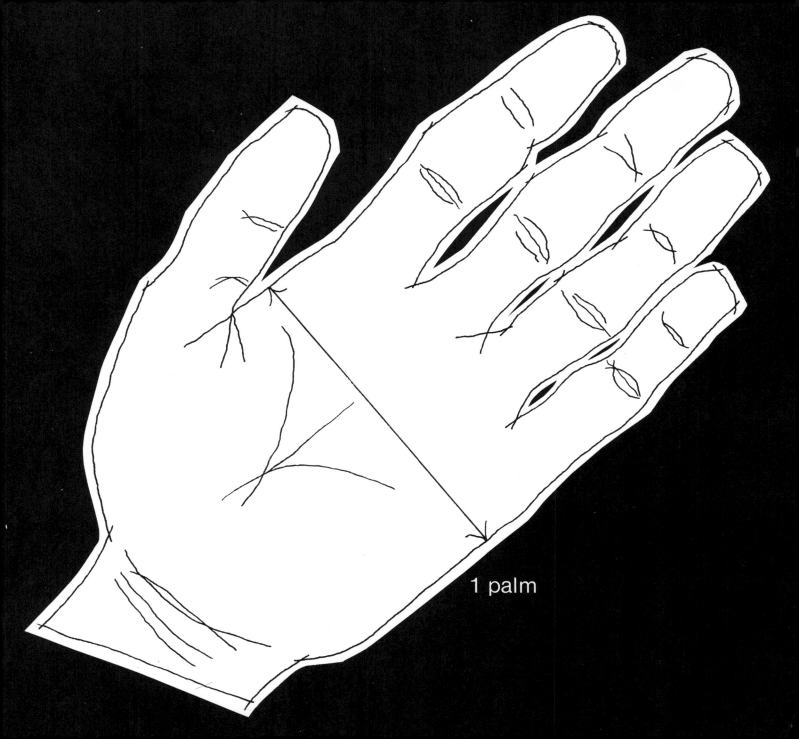

1 palm

At first an INCH was equal to the width of a man's thumb. Then King Edward II of England said, "The length of an inch shall be equal to three grains of barley, dry and round, placed end to end lengthwise."

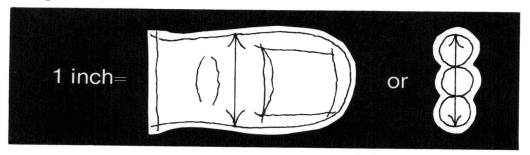

1 inch= or

An old story says that a FOOT was the length of one of the feet of the great French king Charlemagne. But the ancient Greek people, who lived long before Charlemagne, also used a foot-sized unit.

People cannot agree how the YARD began. But a favorite tale says that King Henry I of England fixed the yard as the distance between his nose and the thumb of his outstretched hand.

A HAND was fixed as the width of a good-sized man's hand. It was used long ago to measure the height of horses—and still is!

25

As years passed, many different standard measures began to be used in various parts of the world. It soon became very difficult for people in one country to trade with people in other countries, because each country had its own standard measures.

Then, in 1790, the French people introduced a new system called the metric system. Its basic unit of length is the METER. The new system was easy to use, and soon it spread throughout the world.

Each meter is as long as 100 centimeters. This line segment is 1 CENTIMETER long:

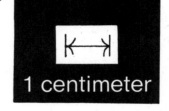

1 centimeter

about 2 centimeters

Cut some sticks 1 centimeter in length. Use them to measure the length of your pencil, your shoe, and your belt. Is a centimeter longer or shorter than a toothpick?

3 meters

Your classroom at school is probably about 3 meters high.

New York

150 kilometers

Philadelphia

For measuring long lengths, the metric system uses KILOMETERS. Each kilometer is made up of 1,000 meters.

The trip from New York City to the city of Philadelphia is about 150 kilometers long.

Meters, centimeters, and kilometers are used by most countries in the world. But in the United States the old system based on lengths of parts of the body has been kept, and it is used by almost everyone. This system uses 4 units. They are inch, foot, yard, and mile.

The smallest of these units of measure is the inch. Cut a string or strip of paper the length of the line segment in the picture.

1 inch |←————————→|

Use it to measure your pencil, your shoe, and your belt. Is an inch longer or shorter than a toothpick? Is it longer or shorter than a centimeter?

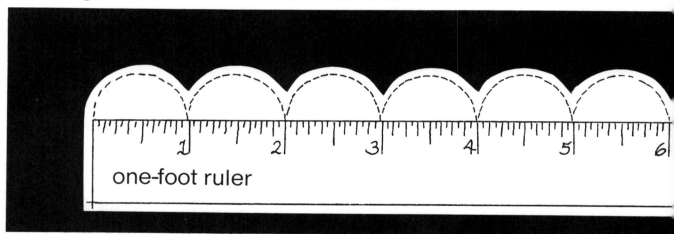

one-foot ruler

There are 12 inches in 1 foot.

There are 36 inches, or 3 feet, in a yard. There are 5,280 feet, or 1,760 yards, in a mile.

A nickel coin is a little less than 1 inch across.

Your classroom at school is probably about 10 feet high.

The trip from New York to Philadelphia is about 90 miles.

Inches, feet, and yards are used as units of measure so often that standard rulers of metal, wood, or plastic are made using these units. Some

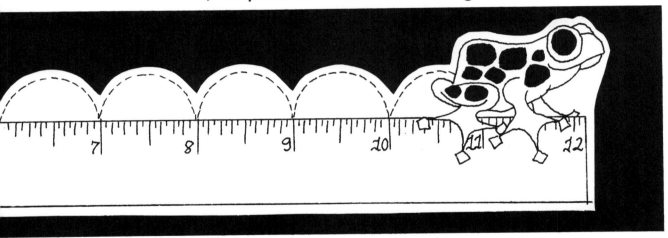

rulers, called "foot rulers," show the length of 12 inches.

Others, called "yardsticks," show the length of 36 inches.

Using these measuring tools, you can find the lengths of any objects you want. If you report the results to someone anywhere in the country, he will know quite clearly what you mean when you say:

"My pencil is longer than 4 inches, but shorter than 5 inches."

or

"My belt is 25 inches long."

or

"My shoe is longer than 7 inches, but shorter than 8 inches."

Get a ruler of your own. There are many things you can measure:

A table.

The television picture tube.

Your height.

Your kite string.

The distance to school.

Can you think of others?

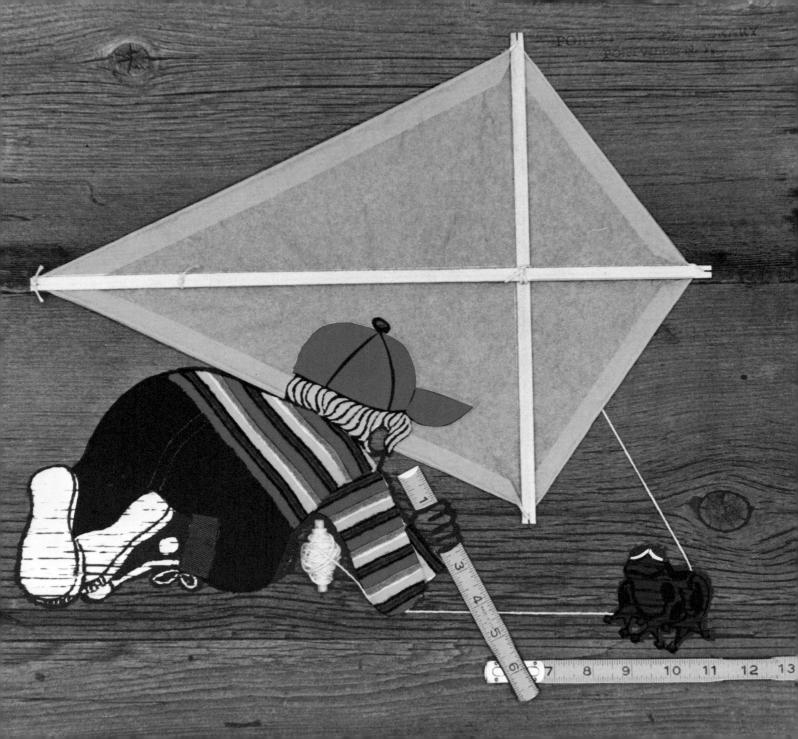

ABOUT THE AUTHOR

Dr. James T. Fey was born, raised, and went to school in Wisconsin Rapids, Wisconsin. He holds degrees from the University of Wisconsin and Columbia University.

Dr. Fey is now assistant professor of mathematics and secondary education at the University of Maryland. He lives in Maryland with his wife and their three-year-old daughter, Ingrid.

ABOUT THE ILLUSTRATOR

Janie Russell was born in Waterloo, Iowa, but moved to Pennsylvania, where she worked as a staff artist at the American Baptist Board of Education while working toward her degree in Graphic Design at the Philadelphia College of Art. She later became the art director for a public relations firm in Devon, Pennsylvania, and eventually started a joint studio with her photographer husband.

Mrs. Russell and her husband make their home in Spring City, Pennsylvania, with their young daughter, who "is a constant source of joy and inspiration." Although she has been doing art and design for children for at least ten years, this is the first children's book Mrs. Russell has illustrated.